BACK TO BASICS

SPELLING

Catherine Hilton and Margaret Hyder

NATIONAL
EXTENSION
COLLEGE

Acknowledgements

© 1993 National Extension College Trust Ltd

Revised 1999. Reprinted 2002 with Assignments included.

ISBN 1 85356 442 7

Written by: Catherine Hilton and Margaret Hyder

Consultants: Michael Charles, Anne Dewsbury, Garth Freeman, Pauline Lawrence, and Margery Styles

Page design by: Squires Graphics

Cover design by: Information Design Workshop.

Printed by: Pear Tree Press Limited, Stevenage

The National Extension College is an educational trust and a registered charity with a distinguished body of trustees. It is an independent, self-financing organisation.

Since it was established in 1963, NEC has pioneered the development of flexible learning for adults. NEC is actively developing innovative materials and systems for distance learning opportunities on over 150 courses, from basic skills to degree and professional training.

For further details of NEC resources and supported courses, contact:

National Extension College
Purbeck Road ,
Cambridge CB2 2HN
Tel. 01223 400200 Fax 01223 400399
Email: info@nec.ac.uk
Website: www.nec.ac.uk

Assignments

If you are studying *Back to Basics: Spelling* with NEC as a course with tutor support then you must refer to the Assignments Booklet that accompanies it. If you are not studying *Back to Basics: Spelling* with NEC and think that you might like to, you can obtain further details by contacting NEC, either in writing at the above address, or by telephoning 01223 400200.

Contents

Links to key skills and basic skills specifications

The units in *Back to Basics Spelling* can be used to develop the skills needed to fulfil these aspects of the Communication Key Skills and City & Guilds Wordpower:

City & Guilds Wordpower Level 2

Unit 308 Communicate in writing: underpinning knowledge and understanding

Proofreading for spelling, punctuation, grammar, accuracy and to make sure instructions have been followed.

City & Guilds Wordpower Level 3

Unit 311 Communicate in writing: underpinning knowledge and understanding

Proofreading for spelling, punctuation, grammar, accuracy of factual content and for following instructions.

Communication Key Skills Level 2 (1995 specifications)

Element 2.2 Produce written material

A student must:

Follow appropriate standard conventions:

    Spelling

Communication Key Skills Level 3 (1995 specifications)

Element 3.2 Produce written material

A student must:

Follow appropriate standard conventions:

    Spelling

Communication Key Skills Level 2 (2000 specifications)

Part A: What you need to know

In writing documents, you need to know how to:

Make meaning clear by writing, proofreading and re-drafting documents so that:

    Words most often used in your work or studies are spelled correctly and spelling of irregular words is checked

Communication Key Skills Level 3 (2000 specifications)

Part A: What you need to know

In writing documents, you need to know how to:

Make meaning clear by writing, proofreading and re-drafting documents so that the following are accurate:

    Spelling

INTRODUCTION

Before you start work on this material you will need:

■ **a notebook.** In several of the units you are asked to note down words with a specific spelling pattern. It is best to use a separate page for each list: it helps to draw your attention to a particular spelling pattern if all the words sharing that pattern are together on a page.

■ a **dictionary** to check spellings and to research words. We suggest a dictionary such as: *Chambers Concise Dictionary, The Concise Oxford Dictionary, The New Penguin English Dictionary* or *Collins New Compact English Dictionary* (make sure that you have the most up-to-date edition).

■ a sheet of A4 paper or card to stop yourself reading the answers to Activities before you have written down your own.

We have tried to keep the technical words in this study guide to a minimum but there are occasions when we have had to use them. You might like to check your understanding of these words before you begin the units. Just write a simple definition of what you think each means and then check each in your dictionary:

■ vowels;

■ consonants;

■ singular;

■ plural;

■ prefixes.

STARTING OUT

Targets

This unit will help you to:

→ consider why spelling is important;

→ assess your own spelling;

→ decide which units you need to study.

Activity

It may be a good starting point to underline any words from the list below that sometimes cause you problems. Then jot down in your notebook any other words whose spelling you feel uncertain about. You may like to look through any past writing you have completed to jog your memory.

suspicious	separate	receive
definite	liaison	sincerely
maintenance	occurring	accommodation
executive	business	undoubtedly
privilege	skilful	thorough
mortgage	miscellaneous	incidentally

As you work through this material you will become aware of other words which cause difficulties for you. Add these to your list as they occur so that you can concentrate on learning words which are important to you.

Thinking about your own spelling

Activity

You have already considered some of your own personal spelling problem areas. However, as it isn't always easy to recall your problem words until you need to use them, you may like to assess your skills further by completing these words. Note that each line (____) may stand for one **or more** letters

transf ____ r ____ d	removed to another place
ex ____ g ____ r ____ t ____	to overstate
ag ____ res ____ i ____ n	hostility
emb ____ r ____ s	to make someone blush
an ____ l ____ s ____ s	a tracing of things to their source, an evaluation
h ____ dr ____ g ____ n	a gas
ac ____ id ____ t ____ l ____ y	by mistake
cas ____ t ____	someone who is injured
____ c ____ r ____ en ____ e	a happening or event
p ____ su ____ d ____	to convince by argument
____ pr ____ s ____	influence or impact
d ____ v ____ r s ____ n	a detour
an ____ r	a response to a question
ext ____ rd ____ n ____ y	not usual
sol ____ n	serious
g ____ t ____ r	a musical instrument
br ____ t ____	to inhale and expel air
ap ____ ro ____ t ____ ly	suitably
v ____ l ____ m ____	a cubic capacity
b ____ c ____ r ____	a cause of infection
mon ____ r c ____	made up of kings and queens
br ____ h ____ re	a pamphlet

(continued overleaf)

m ___ s ___	a place of worship for Muslims
amp ___ i ___ ous	at home on land or water
for ___ n	from abroad
atr ___ c ___ us	dreadful
in ___ t ___ tive	an action that starts something
spe ___ l	not common
___ ord	a combination of notes played together
___ r ___ sti ___ t y	a religion
eq ___ l ___ t ___ r ___ l	with all sides equal
parl ___ m ___ t	an assembly which makes or passes laws

You can check your answers by turning to page 9.

If you have made mistakes, think about the type of mistakes you have made. There may be a pattern to your errors. Having spotted the type of spelling mistakes you are likely to make, you will be able to work on those and study the units that deal with them. There is more help with this on the next page.

You can also look at the underlined words in the first activity of this unit and those you wrote in your notebook earlier in this unit. See if you can analyse your problem areas in those words too. Make a note of these in your notebook, like this:

PROBLEM AREAS

Making mistakes with double letters – I never know whether there

should be a double or single letter in certain words.

Review

You may decide to work through all of the following units or you may prefer to target those units which deal with your particular spelling concerns. Use the following diagram to help identify the units you need to work on in particular.

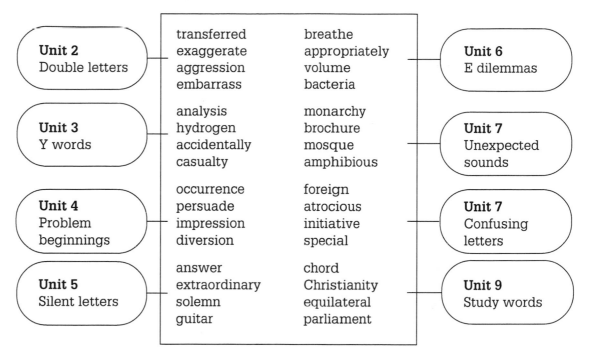

Whichever way of working you choose, you will find that:

- The advice given in one unit complements and extends that given in another.

- Certain words do not conveniently fall into just one area but often contain several different elements. Here are some examples:

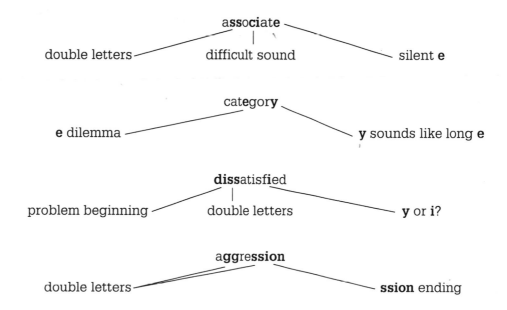

Good luck with the work you are now going to carry out. Thinking about your spelling problems is a positive step – the first step along the road to improvement.

UNIT 2

DOUBLE LETTERS

Targets

This unit will help you to:

➜ consider why double letters can cause problems;

➜ look at some of the occasions when double letters occur in words;

➜ find out ways of dealing with double letters.

Most of us have problems with double letters in words at some time or other. How often have you written the word **occasion**, paused to look at it and wondered whether there are:

■ two **c**s and one **s**

■ two **c**s and two **s**s

■ one **c** and two **s**s

■ one **c** and one **s**?

The longer you think about it, the more confused you can become until all the versions look wrong.

Many everyday words have double letters in them. Some of the most straightforward include:

better	calling
written	suffer
rabbit	suggest
funny	address
manner	tomorrow

Here are some longer words with double letters which you may have trouble with:

exaggerate	attraction
according	traveller
committee	approach
attempt	faithfully
permission	illustrated
immediate	excellent
thankfully	proceed
possess	disappoint

Activity

> You may be aware of specific words with double letters that you are sometimes uncertain about. We suggest you list these in your notebook. You can add to your list as other examples occur to you, either while you are working through this unit or later when you are studying other units.

How to tackle double letters

In the rest of this unit we're going to suggest six ways of tackling double letters. These include:

- looking at words more carefully;
- splitting words up into parts;
- seeing a smaller word within the longer word;
- devising chants;
- learning rules;
- grouping words together.

Looking at words more carefully

We said at the beginning of this unit that often when you write a word like **occasion**, you can look at it and think it looks wrong.

What can you do?

- If you write a word with a double letter and it looks wrong, try writing it with a single letter. Does it look better?
- If you've written it with a single letter and it doesn't look right, try a double letter.
- You can then use your dictionary to check.
- You have already started making a list of the double letter words that cause you trouble. Work on these words one at a time, using the following plan:

> Copy the word carefully.
>
> Underline the double or single letter.
>
> Concentrate on this part of the word as you write it from memory.

- When you come across such words in your reading, pause and really look at them so that you notice the pattern of single or double letters.

Split words up into parts

By doing this you can emphasise double letters: bet/ter fun/ny rab/bit.

Each of these words has two parts. After dividing the word in two at the double letter, you can say each part aloud, emphasising the last letter of the first part and the first letter of the second part. For example, **bet/ter** draws your attention to the repeated **t**.

This strategy can also work with some longer and less straightforward words:

ap/pet/ite ef/fec/tive cur/ric/u/lum.

Activity

Practise splitting up these words in a similar way. As you do so, think of each part as taking one effort of breath. Make sure there is a split between the double letters.

apparent	questionnaire	personnel
accredited	opposite	impossible
transferring	terrorist	immaculate
disarray	beginning	illogical

See smaller words within a longer word

The word **fallible** means 'liable to make a mistake. It sounds as if it could apply to us all!

If you are worried about whether it has one or two **l**s, concentrate on the word **fall** at the beginning. This should help you remember the double **l**.

Activity

In each of the words below see if you can spot the short word of which the double letters form a part.

intelligence	assailant	usually	labelled
alliance	impassable	parallel	excellence

Did you find: tell, ass, all, bell, all, pass, all, cell, in this order going from left to right across the lines?

Consider using this strategy to help you with any double letter words you encounter.

Devise chants

We remember **occasion** by having chanted to ourselves: two **c**s and an **s**.

recommend = one **c** and two **m**s

committee = two **m**s, two **t**s, and two **e**s – two of everything!

Activity

See if this method helps you. Compose a chant for each of these words:

cassette	committed	accommodate
necessary	commissioned	successfully

Don't worry if you don't find this helpful; it may even confuse you! We all have our own ways of remembering words. It's up to you to work out which ways are best for you.

Learn rules

Here are two rules; you may have heard them before.

> When you add **ly** to the end of a word, add it on to the complete word. Don't take any letters off the word. For example, **accidental** + **ly** = **accidentally**.
>
> With words that end in l, this results in two **ls** appearing together, so:
>
> professionally   successfully   especially
>
> specifically   usually   virtually

> When you add a prefix to a word, put it on the whole word. Don't miss out any letters. For example, **dis** + **satisfy** = **dissatisfy**.
>
> So:
>
> dissimilar   illegal   unnatural
>
> immobile   innumerate   irresponsible

By the way

■ There are other rules which also help you with double letters in words. You may want to research these rules by studying more detailed books about spelling. A list of such books is given on p. 48.

■ Unit 4 tells you more about prefixes.

Grouping words together

By looking at 'families' of words, you can appreciate the pattern for that particular family. Here are some examples:

associate	associated	associating	association	
profess	professor	profession	professional	professionally
total	totalling	totalled		
quarrel	quarrelling	quarrelled		
rebel	rebelling	rebelled	rebellion	rebellious
equip	equipping	equipped		

Review

In this unit we have tried to draw your attention to words which may be difficult for you because they have:

■ double letters where you may be tempted to write a single letter;

■ a single letter where you might expect a double letter.

We hope that the strategies we have suggested will make it easier to deal with such words. We realise that some strategies may be more helpful than others, so concentrate on those that suit you.

UNIT 3

Y WORDS

Targets

This unit will help you to:

→   identify times when the letter **y** may cause confusion;

→   recognise the occasions when **y** has different sounds;

→   deal with words ending in **y**.

Why can y be confusing?

In this unit we look at some of the occasions when **y** may cause you difficulties. You have probably noticed that **y** can have different sounds in different words. Compare these two lists:

yesterday	secretar**y**
youthful	accessor**y**
yeast	anniversar**y**.

In the left hand list **y** has its consonant sound (that's the sound you expect it to make), but in the right-hand list **y** sounds more like **e** (the long **e** sound you hear at the beginning of **even**). We'll be studying the different sounds that **y** has and some strategies for coping with this in the next section of this unit.

You may also have noticed that words which end in **y** tend not to follow the usual spelling patterns. For example, when we want to make a word plural, we usually add **s** but in words ending in **y** this isn't always true. So:

calendar	→	calendars
turkey	→	turkeys
but company	→	companies.

If you are uncertain why some **y** words don't seem to follow the usual patterns when endings are added, you'll find help on page 16.

Other y sounds

You have already seen that **y** can have a **y** or an **e** sound, but it can also have other sounds.

For example, in **hydrofoil** the **y** makes an **i** sound as in the word **Iceland** – this is what we call a long **i** sound. In **cylinder** the **y** makes what is called a short **i** sound like the sound at the beginning of the word **is**.

Activity

Read the following words aloud and decide which sound the **y** makes in each word.

1 stationar**y**	2 enc**y**clopaedia	3 criticall**y**
4 c**y**linder	5 s**y**mpathetic	6 h**y**giene
7 entirel**y**	8 h**y**steria	9 letharg**y**

You should have identified the **y** in (1), (3), (7) and (9) as having a long **e** sound and in words (2) and (6) as having a long **i** sound. In the remaining words the **y** has a short **i** sound.

By the way

Recognising the different sounds of **y** can help you on the occasions when you are uncertain about whether to use a **y**, an **i** or an **e**. If a word looks wrong spelt with either an **i** or an **e**, try writing it again with a **y** and see if that looks right. Then check in a dictionary.

Another strategy that may help you is learning where the different sounds for **y** are most likely to occur in words.

Activity

Study the words in the box below and then complete the statements about **y** sounds that follow.

warrant**y**	letharg**y**	**y**ield	def**y**
d**y**spepsia	c**y**clone	fallac**y**	disparit**y**
multipl**y**	entirel**y**	suitabilit**y**	ph**y**sics
h**y**steria	lar**y**nx	s**y**mmetr**y**	brewer**y**

The consonant **y** sound occurs

A long **i** sound is most likely to occur

A long **e** sound usually occurs

A short **i** sound occurs mostly

Use the following notes to check your answer:

■ When **y** is the first letter of a word it has a consonant **y** sound.

■ A **y** can sound like a long **i** near the beginning, in the middle or at the end of a word.

■ A **y** at the end of words often sounds like a long **e**. This is especially helpful when you hear a **tee** or **lee** sound at the end of a word – it will probably be made by **ty** or **ly**.

■ A **y** can have a short **i** sound near the beginning of a word or in the middle of a word.

You may find it difficult to remember all this. If you know that you often have difficulty with **y** sounds in words, list the words you find most difficult to spell. Using the help you've been given, try to identify which sound the **y** is making and then find a way of remembering the spelling pattern.

Do you need s or ies?

At the beginning of this unit we showed you two words which ended in **y** (**company** and **turkey**) which become **companies** and **turkeys** in the plural. Here are two more words which end in **y**:

rela**y**	rela**ys**
deput**y**	deput**ies**

Activity

Look at the letter before the **y** in **relay** and **deputy** and then try to explain why there is this difference in spelling when you make each word plural.

We hope you noticed that if the letter before the final **y** in a word is a vowel (a,e,i,o,u) you add an **s**, but if the letter before the **y** is a consonant you have to change the **y** to an **i** and then add **es**.

Activity

If this idea is new to you, give yourself some further practice by writing the plurals of the words given below. Then check whether your answers are correct by consulting your dictionary.

boundary	cemetery	alloy	tragedy
scarcity	emergency	itinerary	casualty
chimney	survey	burglary	volley
valley			

Other endings

We hope that you now feel more confident writing the plural of words ending in **y**. You will find that similar rules apply when you add on other endings to **y** words:

occu**py**

+ ed ➜ occup**ied**

+ er ➜ occup**ier**

(Note the consonant before the final **y**.)

but

sur**vey**

+ ed ➜ survey**ed**

+ or ➜ survey**or**

(Note the vowel before the final **y**.)

Before you tackle the next activity, remember that you cannot change a final **y** to **i** if the ending being added starts with an **i**. So, for example:

satis**fy**   +   ing   ➜   satis**fying**   (Keep the **y**.)

Activity

Practise this by adding the ending shown in brackets to each word. Make a note of those in which **y** changes to **i**.

1 scurry (ed)	5 secretary (al)	9 necessary (ly)
2 rally (ing)	6 envy (able)	10 journey (ing)
3 clumsy (ness)	7 luxury (ant)	11 rusty (er)
4 weary (some)	8 purvey (ing)	12 supply (ing)

You should have changed the **y** to an **i** in (1), (3), (4), (5), (6), (7), (9) and (11). In the other words the **y** is kept unchanged when the ending is added. Look back to the examples above if you had any difficulty with this activity.

Review

Now check back to the targets at the beginning of this unit. You should have a clearer idea of when **y** can be confused with either an **e** or an **i** and why adding an ending can affect the spelling of a word which ends in **y**. Also, you will probably be more aware of which **y** words cause you trouble. It would be a good idea to add these to your notebook so that you can practise them.

PROBLEM BEGINNINGS

Targets

This unit will help you to:

→ think more carefully about the beginnings of words;

→ identify word beginnings that you need to work on;

→ develop strategies for dealing with tricky word beginnings.

You may sometimes feel that it is the middle part or the end of a word that causes you the biggest headache. But if you are uncertain about how a word starts you might not even be able to check it in a dictionary! In this unit we will be looking at some of those word beginnings that may trip you up.

Unclear beginnings

As you work through this section we'll be inviting you to pinpoint the sounds made by the letters at the beginnings of words. You'll probably find it easiest to hear the exact sound if you say the word or word beginnings aloud.

Is it de or di?

These two beginnings often sound very similar.

Activity

Below we list some **de** and **di** words in which the **e** or the **i** is missing. Fill in the missing letter. If you are uncertain, try writing the word both ways and see which looks right. You should then check it in a dictionary.

1 d _e_ ficient	8 d _i_ minish	15 d _e_ sease
2 d _e_ ffuse	9 d _i_ fuse	16 d _i_ sist
3 d _e_ spise	10 d _i_ scerning	17 d _i_ sperse
4 d _e_ srupt	11 d _e_ lusion	18 d _i_ linquent
5 d _e_ ciduous	12 d _e_ sparaging	19 d _i_ sastrous
6 d _i_ ffident	13 d _e_ sperate	20 d _e_ liberate
7 d _i_ spel	14 d _e_ scription	21 d _e_ stroy

Numbers (1), (3), (5), (9), (11), (13), (14), (16), (18), (20) and (21) start with **de**; the others have a
di beginning. If you made any mistakes, you'll need to make a note of any of the words you feel are important for you to learn. You'll also need to find a way that will help you to learn them.

What can you do?

- Every time you write the word, emphasise in your head the **de** or **di** beginning.

- Check whether the words you had difficulty with fall into any special patterns. Was it, for example, only **des** words that you found difficult? If so, group the words together and learn them in families. For example:

destroy **des**troying **des**troyer **des**truction.

Or put the words into a memorable sentence:

He **des**pised the **des**perate **des**troyers.

Deciduous trees lose their leaves **e**very winter.

Is it pur or per?

Have you ever written the word **pursue** and then wondered if it is spelt 'persue', or written **persuade** and then tried it again as 'pursuade'? It's not always easy to be sure which is correct. (In both of these cases it was the first alternative.)

What can you do?

Here are two ways of tackling this difficulty:

- There are more **per** words than **pur** so if you are in doubt check in your dictionary under **per** first.

- There are so few common **pur** words that you could group them all together in one memorable sentence. (You will find the most common **pur** words in the activity below.)

 # Activity

Check how many **pur** and **per** words you already know by writing either **u** or **e** in the space in each word below. Look up each word in a dictionary to check whether it is correct.

p __ rmanent	p __ rge	p __ rspire
p __ rpose	p __ rplex	p __ rsevere
p __ rchase	p __ rple	p __ rsistant
p __ rpetual	p __ rsecute	

Is it in or im?

An **in** sound is easily confused with an **im** sound.

Should a judge be **im**partial or **in**partial? (The correct word is **impartial**, meaning that he or she doesn't take sides in a case.)

Activity

Look at the pattern shown in these **in** and **im** words. Can you see which letters are likely to follow **in** and which are likely to follow **im**?

inflammable	incompetent	intimate
insipid	intrepid	inflate
informal	inhospitable	indulge
inefficient	inhumane	intact

immobile	impertinent	impotent
impress	immoral	imprint
immense	impact	implore
impose	immortal	impede

Write your ideas here.

In can be followed by

Im is usually only followed by

We hope you noticed the pattern for **im** beginnings – **im** is found mostly before **m**s or **p**s. If the next letter isn't either of these, then the word probably starts with **in**.

Review

Now that you have seen examples of troublesome word beginnings and found practical ways of coping with them, you should feel that you have achieved the targets for this unit. Clearly we have not been able to cover every type of problem beginning in one unit, but you will be able to collect more examples as your work continues.

UNIT
5

SILENT LETTERS

Targets

This unit will help you to:

→ become more aware of silent letters and silent word parts;

→ anticipate when silent letters are most likely to occur;

→ find useful ways of dealing with silent letters.

You are probably aware of letters in words which are seen but not heard. Some letters of the alphabet are more likely to be silent than others, depending on their:

■ position in words;

■ combination with other letters.

Being aware of silent letters

At this stage it would be useful to consider what you already know about silent letters. Make a list in your notebook of words that have silent letters in them. Underline any of these words that cause you problems. We'll come back to your list later in the unit so that you can note down any other words that you feel you would like to concentrate on.

Activity

A silent letter (or letters) is missing from each of the words in the box below. It's easy to see what each word is because the silent letter isn't needed in the pronunciation of the word. The challenge is to spell them correctly!

__ neumonia	__ onourable	g __ ess
condem __	__ hole	play __ right
sle __ ge	s __ enario	dou __ tful
__ nome	receiv __	yo __ k
i __ land	__ nowledge	cau __ __ t
bris __ le	hym __	__ i __ le

Working from left to right across the columns, the following letters are silent: p, h, u; n, w, w; d, c, b; g, e, l; s, k, gh; t, n, a and s.

When are letters likely to be silent?

Activity

Each of the panels below and opposite shows a pattern of when you would expect a letter to be silent. See if you can decide which of the following explanations each column corresponds to:

K is silent before **n** at the beginning of words.

G is silent before **n**.

T is silent before **ch**.

C is silent after **s**.

D is silent before **ge**.

B can be silent either at the end of or in the middle of words.

U following **g** is silent when it occurs before the vowels **a**, **e**, **i**.

Gh can be silent at the end of or within words.

W is silent before **r**.

There are also spaces for some missing examples which you may like to complete – a dictionary will help you with some of the patterns. If you cannot complete all the examples now, come back to this activity when you have finished the rest of this unit as further examples will appear later in the unit.

1
kitchen

Dutch

clutch

butcher

_____

_____

_____

2
daughter

haughty

although

neighbour

_____

_____

_____

3
gnaw

gnarl

campaign

reign

poignant

_____

_____

4
scent

science

descent

scythe

rescind

_____

_____

5
wrong

written

wrinkle

_____

_____

_____

_____

6
hedge

sludge

wedge

fledgling

_____

_____

_____

(continued opposite)

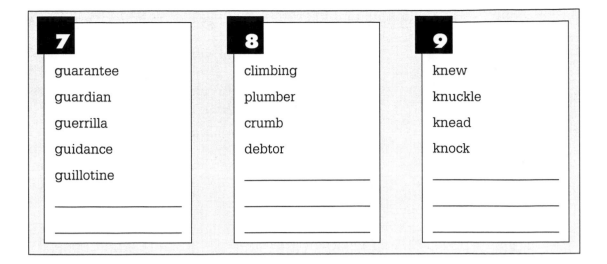

7	**8**	**9**
guarantee	climbing	knew
guardian	plumber	knuckle
guerrilla	crumb	knead
guidance	debtor	knock
guillotine		
_____	_____	_____
_____	_____	_____
	_____	_____

Activity

Here are some further examples of silent letters. See if you can circle the silent letter (or, in a few cases, letters) in each of these words – but be warned: not all fit into a pattern!

wretch	autumn	pneumatic	rhyme
ghost	ploughman	whining	numbness
dough	judgement	salmon	whether
sketch	exhibition	rhapsody	psychic
badger	receipt	Wednesday	rhubarb
heir	rhetoric	gauge	brought
scratch	subtle	grudge	deceive
biscuit	design	solemn	listen
ghastly	tomb	valuable	column

Did you notice all the silent letters? Working across the columns from left to right the letters were: w, n, p and e, h;   h, gh, h, b;   gh, d (e), l, h;   t, h, h, p and h;   d, p, d, h; h, h, u (e), gh;   t, b, d (e), e;   u, g, n, t;   gh, b, a, n.

As you spotted each silent letter, you may have noticed some more patterns:

> **H** is silent after **g** at the beginnings of words.
>
> **H** is silent after **r** at the beginnings of words.
>
> **H** is silent after **w** at the beginnings of words.
>
> **H** is silent after **m** at the ends of words.

If there are any words in this activity that you feel uncertain of spelling correctly, add them to the list in your notebook so that you can work on them too.

What can you do about silent letters?

- You may remember the chef in an advert for Knorr's stock cubes on television. He couldn't tell the difference between his own stock and Knorr's stock, but he could spell Knorr because he remembered '**K**-norr has the **k**-now-how!' Pronouncing and emphasising the silent letter will draw attention to the letter and help you to spell the word correctly.

- If you are aware of the probable pattern for silent letters in words, you are more likely to remember to put the problem letter or letters in when you spell the word.

- If you have a problem with a silent letter in a particular word, see if you can find other words like it so that you can group words together which share the same pattern.

You may already have other ways of dealing with words which have silent letters in them. If so, make a note of these below.

Review

You should now be on the alert for silent letters or word parts, and have a clearer idea of where these are likely to occur. We hope that as a result you will be able to deal with these more effectively in your spelling.

By becoming aware of which words contain silent letters you will find it much easier to use your dictionary. If you didn't know that **p** could sometimes be silent at the beginning of words, you might never be able to find words such as **psalm**, **pseudonym**, **psychology** or **ptarmigan**!

UNIT 6

E DILEMMAS

Targets

This unit will help you to:

→ establish why **e** can cause problems;

→ identify the letters which can make an **e** sound in words;

→ devise ways of remembering words where an **e** may cause confusion.

Over the years many students have complained to us that the letter **e** and an **e** sound can make the spelling of certain words difficult. To **e** or not to **e** – that is the question!

By an **e** sound, we are thinking of the sound that the letter **e** makes in words such as **evening** or **emu**. This is sometimes referred to as a 'long' **e** sound, in contrast to the 'short' **e** sound in words such as **met** and **end**.

Why is e difficult?

The letter **e** can cause difficulties because:

■ It is sometimes silent.

■ It may be tempting to include it even if it isn't needed.

■ It can sound like another vowel.

Activity

Perhaps you are already aware of **e** words that trouble you. If so, write them in your notebook. You will then be able to refer to them when you are studying this unit and match each with the relevant advice about how to deal with **e** words.

Now let's look at each of the four difficulties in turn.

When e is silent

Activity

Look carefully at the words in the box below and try to draw up a list of patterns for when **e** may be silent at the ends of words. Make a note of these on a separate sheet.

engin**e**	catalogu**e**	damag**e**
precis**e**	immers**e**	continu**e**
uniqu**e**	bandag**e**	concis**e**
intelligenc**e**	exchang**e**	brows**e**
expens**e**	vagu**e**	advic**e**
venu**e**	absenc**e**	techniqu**e**

You may have noticed that **e** is frequently silent in words:

■ ending in **ce** when the **ce** makes an **s** sound

■ ending with **ge** where the **ge** makes a **j** sound

■ ending with **se** where the last sound you hear in a word is an **s**

■ ending in **ue**.

It can also occur at the end of other words which don't follow these patterns, for example:

pressur**e**	procedur**e**	decisiv**e**	freez**e**
definit**e**	enquir**e**	excit**e**	decid**e**

The letter **e** may also be silent in other positions in words. The following activity will help you to appreciate this.

Activity

Put a tick above the spelling which is correct in each case.

mathematics/mathmatics	severly/severely
management/managment	bachlor/bachelor
sincerely/sincerly	definitly/definitely
completely/completly	securly/securely
advertisement/advertisment	ninty/ninety

In the first column the first word of the pair is correct. In the second column the second word in each pair is correct.

What can you do?

In Unit 5, 'Silent Letters', we suggested that you could sound out the silent letter in a word as if it were meant to be pronounced. But it isn't easy to do this with the letter **e**. Here are two alternative suggestions:

■ Look at any word with an **e** that causes you problems and underline the **e** to draw it to your attention. Then test yourself by writing the word from memory.

■ Refer to detailed spelling books to learn the rules about **e** – rules such as:

*If a word ends in a silent **e**, you keep this **e** when you add an ending which begins with a consonant.*

This rule accounts for words such as:

unfortunate – unfortunat**e**ly	immaculate – immaculat**e**ly
extreme – extrem**e**ly	safe – saf**e**ty
lone – lon**e**some	spite – spit**e**ful

Although there are some exceptions to this rule, it and others about **e** can help you to decide whether an **e** is needed or not.

The unnecessary e

Activity

Look carefully at each pair of words in the box below and tick the one that you think is correct.

1	interprete/interpret	10	enquiring/enquireing
2	umberella/umbrella	11	exciteable/excitable
3	develop/develope	12	argument/arguement
4	writeing/writing	13	embarrass/embarrasse
5	enrolement/enrolment	14	enthrale/enthral
6	exaggerateing/exaggerating	15	icey/icy
7	wintery/wintry	16	schemeing/scheming
8	truely/truly	17	valuable/valueable
9	enterance/entrance	18	wondrous/wonderous

In numbers (3), (10), (12), (13), (17) and (18) the first word in each pair is correct; in the rest of the examples the second word in each pair is correct.

By the way

There are some words which can be spelt either way – with or without an **e**. For example:

likeable/likable   loveable/lovable   sizeable/sizable

judgement/judgment   acknowledgement/acknowledgment.

In these cases the choice is up to you.

What can you do?

■ Learn the rules about **e**, for example:

*When you add an ending which begins with a vowel to a word ending in **e**, you usually drop the final **e** from the word.*

reverse → reversal   achieve → achieving   fame → famous.

Although there are some exceptions, this is a useful rule.

■ Make a note of any words which tend to cause you difficulties and practise these regularly until you are certain of the spelling.

■ Use personal memory aids, for example:

Develop ends in **lop**: think of trees being lopped down to build a new supermarket!

Umbrella has only three parts: um/brel/la (umberella would have four).

'It was a **truly icy** and **wintry** day' (**true, ice, winter** all drop an **e** when they become **truly, icy, wintry**).

The letter 'i' may sound like e

English vowels often create uncertainties in spelling. There are words that people misspell by putting in an **e** when the long **e** sound is made by an **i**, for example:

serious   audio   litre   imperial

ingenious   evidence   deteriorated   auditorium

What can you do?

■ As you will have seen, the vowel **i** can sound like an **e** in some words. By being aware of this you won't automatically use an **e**: you will consider an **i** in certain words.

■ Imagine yourself altering the pronunciation of the word to emphasise its spelling – for example, in **serious**, stress a *short* **i** sound.

Review

Put your learning in this unit into practice by completing the spelling of these words (one space represents one letter). If you are uncertain about a particular word, go back over the unit and see if it fits one of the patterns we've looked at.

p __ rs __ __	to follow
th __ __ __ __	a likely explanation
lon __ __ __ n __ __ s	a feeling of being isolated
pr __ j __ __ __ c __	an unfair feeling for or against
p __ __ c __ d __ __ __	a course of action
__ her __ __ s	but on the other hand
ex __ __ __ m __ __y	very
n __ t __ __ __ ab __ __	able or likely to be seen
th __ __ __ f __ r __	consequently
q __ __ __ __	to wait in a line
de __ __ c __ __ __ __ y	tenderly

Check your response:

pursue, theory, loneliness, prejudice, procedure, whereas, extremely, noticeable, therefore, queue, delicately.

UNEXPECTED SOUNDS

Targets

This unit will help you to:

→ recognise some letter combinations that make unexpected sounds;

→ practise spelling such words;

→ develop your vocabulary by introducing you to some words which may be new to you.

In this unit you will be looking at a variety of words which students sometimes find troublesome because they contain a letter combination that makes an unexpected sound. Each section within this unit deals with a different unexpected sound. You may find it helpful to work through the following activity to see whether you need to focus on any specific section.

Activity

Add the missing letters to each of these words and then spot which sound the missing letters make each time.

word	meaning	sound
1 pro ____ et	a person who predicts the future	
2 an ____ or	a heavy hooked device	
3 obli ____	slanting	

You may have seen that the sounds were: (1), f; (2), k; (3), k. The letters which made these sounds were: **f** sound – **ph**; **k** sound – **ch**; **k** sound – **que**. You may now wish to work through the whole unit or you may prefer to concentrate on only those sounds and letter combinations which you found difficult to identify.

Unexpected f sounds

Activity

Look at these words which, as you can see, all contain an **f** sound. Sort the words into four groups according to which letter or letters make the **f** sound.

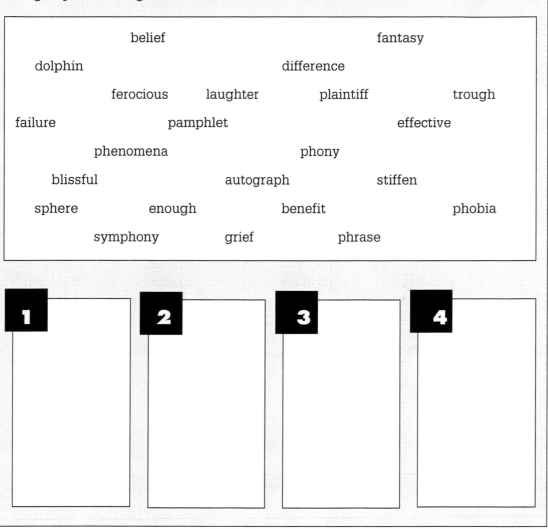

belief   fantasy

dolphin   difference

ferocious   laughter   plaintiff   trough

failure   pamphlet   effective

phenomena   phony

blissful   autograph   stiffen

sphere   enough   benefit   phobia

symphony   grief   phrase

1	**2**	**3**	**4**

Check by reading the following statements about the **f** sound in words and then deciding which of your four groups could be given as an example:

- **Ff** makes an **f** sound in the middle and at the end of words but never at the beginning of a word (except in some family names).

- **Gh** can make a **f** sound in the middle or at the end of a word but not at the beginning.

- **F** makes an **f** sound at the beginning, in the middle or at the end of a word.

- **Ph** can make an **f** sound at the beginning, in the middle or at the end of a word.

By the way

Words in which **ph** makes an **f** sound come from the Greek language. Many of these words have a medical or scientific meaning. Examples include:

physics   pharmacy   phial   phosphorus.

Activity

Now try completing the following **ph** words. You should then check the spelling of each word in a dictionary.

tri _ _ _ _ _	a victory or success
dol _ _ _ _ _	a sea mammal
auto _ _ _ _ _ _	a signature
ne _ _ _ _ _	a family relation
hy _ _ _ _	a punctuation point
em _ _ _ _ _ _ _	to stress a sound or word
gra _ _ _ _ _	very descriptive
gra _ _ _ _ _ _	used in pencil lead

What can you do?

Although you won't need to learn every **ph** word noted in this unit, you will need to find a way of learning those you personally find useful. Here are some suggestions:

■ **Ph** words often form memorable word families, for example:

photo – words that are all to do with light:

photograph   **ph**otocopy   **ph**otosynthesis.

■ When you practise spelling **ph** words, underline the **ph** to emphasise the letter combination.

■ Try breaking the word into parts between the **p** and the **h** and emphasising the separate sounds in your head, for example:

sphere – sp   here   ('here' also forms a word)

graphic – grap   hic

Unexpected k sounds

A **k** sound is usually made by:

k	**k**ennel	than**k**
c	**c**ash	pani**c**
ck	sa**ck**	ja**ck**et

However, sometimes the **k** sound is made by **que** or **ch**:

me**ch**anic	anti**que**
e**ch**o	mysti**que**
chord	techni**que**

Activity

Look at the position within each word of the **ch** and **que** in the box below. What do you notice about the **que** words shown in the box? Make a note below:

What do you notice about the **ch** words? Again, make a note:

You will have seen that the letter combination **que** making a **k** sound is only at the end of a word. The combination **ch** making a **k** sound can be at the beginning of a word or in the middle, but not at the end. Let's look more closely at each combination.

The sounds of ch

Activity

Say each of these **ch** words aloud. Make a note of the different sounds that **ch** represents.

cheer	check	chemical
cholesterol		chauffeur
ache	chilblain	chronicle
technical	cherub	chlorophyll
churlish	school	chastise

The letter combination **ch** makes:

■ its usual **ch** sound (as in the word **church**) in cheer, check, chilblain, cherub, churlish and chastise;

■ a **k** sound in chemical, ache, chronicle, technical, cholesterol, chlorophyll and school;

■ a **sh** sound in chauffeur.

33

Activity

You may like to find further examples where the **ch** makes a **k** sound. Use a dictionary to find at least six words which start in this way. Note them below.

When we tried this activity we found: chaos, chemist, character, Christmas, choir, choral, charisma, choreograph, chromatic, chromosome, chronic, chronometer, chrysanthemum.

Remembering que words

Activity

Practise the spelling of the following **que** words by writing the correct word for each meaning. We have given you the first letter each time. Remember that the **que** combination comes at the end of a word. Use your dictionary if necessary.

g _ _ _ _ _ _ _ _   particularly ugly or distorted

u _ _ _ _ _ _   being the only one of its kind

o _ _ _ _ _ _   not transparent

p _ _ _ _ _ _ _ _ _ _   like a picture

t _ _ _ _ _ _ _ _ _   method of carrying out a task

p _ _ _ _ _ _ _   bodily shape

o _ _ _ _ _ _   slanting

Starting from the bottom of the box you should have found these words: oblique, physique, technique, picturesque, opaque, unique, grotesque.

Review

As a reminder of the points and strategies we've covered in this unit, try identifying the unexpected letter combination in each of the words in the box below. Then, if you feel unsure of a spelling, try to find a way to remember it.

phantom	orchestra
stomach	catastrophe

UNIT 8

CONFUSING LETTERS

Targets

This unit will help you to:

→ identify some more unusual ways of making a sibilant sound within words;

→ explain various sounds that the letters **ie** and **ei** can make within words;

→ find strategies to deal with these difficult spelling patterns.

Sibilant sounds

A sibilant sound is a hissing or buzzing sound, like the one made by the consonants **s**, **x** and **z**. Here are some examples:

such   success   six   fez   zebra   sex.

Activity

There are also combinations of letters that can make a sibilant sound. Look at the words below and put a ring round the letters which go together to make a sibilant sound.

officer	retention	fuzziness	citizen
gush	fussy	ceiling	relation
shower	catch	cycle	commercial
shallow	cyclamen	mention	century
buzz	vicious	scratch	pencil
chance	harsh	choice	facing

You have probably ringed the combinations: sh, ss, tch, zz, ch, ce, ci, cy, ti.

The individual letters and the pairs of letters make similar but not identical hissing sounds. Knowing about this variety of possibilities can help you when you are uncertain about the spelling of a word. If the word looks wrong with one letter or combination of letters, you can try other possibilities until the spelling looks right.

Making sh sounds

This is the sound you utter if you want to keep someone quiet! In many words it's quite straightforward as it's spelt **sh** just as you would expect it to be, for example:

shambles   reshape   shoal   shoulder.

However, people often find words in which **ti, ci, xi, si** and **ssi** are pronounced **sh** more difficult to deal with. Examples of the first three include:

patient   ancient   precious   torrential   impression

patience   sufficient   efficient   anxious.

What can you do?

Your spelling may be more successful if you bear in mind that:

- **Ci** is more common than **ti** in these types of words.

- **Xi** as in anxious is an unusual pattern.

Activity

> Decide whether to use **ci** or **ti** in these words. If you are uncertain, try each in turn and see which looks better.
>
> | | | | |
> |---|---|---|---|
> | influen _ti_ al | superfi _ci_ al | pre _ci_ ous | par _ci_ al |
> | residen _ti_ al | suspi _ci_ ous | spa _ti_ al | essen _ti_ al |
> | ini _ci_ al | confiden _ti_ al | espe _ci_ ally | so _ci_ al |
> | offi _ci_ al | politi _ci_ an | deli _ci_ ous | musi _ci_ an |

Going across the columns, from left to right, you should have suggested: influential, superficial, precious, partial, residential, suspicious, spatial, essential, initial, confidential, especially, social, official, politician, delicious, musician.

Shun sounds

The sound we are going to look at now sounds exactly like the word **shun**, meaning 'to ignore or stay away from'. It can be made by:

tion   sion   ssion.

Examples include:

fascination   mansion   profession

congratulation   tension   succession.

What can you do?

You'll find it easier to select the right ending if you bear in mind that:

- Many more words end in **tion** than **sion** or **ssion**.

- Many of the words ending in **ssion** are formed from a word which already ends in **ss**, for example: succe**ss** → succe**ssion**.

Activity

See if you can choose the correct ending for each of these words. When you've written the word, check it by consulting your dictionary.

permi _tion_	suspen _ce_	cancella _sion_
pen _cil_	occa _sion_	co-opera _tive_
se _faction_	exhibi _tion_	omi _____
satisfac _tion_	competi _tion_	aggre _sive_
destruc _tion_	suppre _sion_	fu _____
repre _sion_	revi _sion_	crea _tion_
televi _sion_	celebra _tion_	preci _ous_

Going across the columns you will have added on the following endings: ssion, sion, tion; sion, sion, tion; ssion, tion, ssion; tion, tion, ssion; tion, ssion, sion; ssion, sion, tion; sion, tion, sion.

By the way

■ Here are some unusual words with a **shun** ending:

complexion   ocean   suspicion   cushion   fashion.

If these are words you feel unsure about, it's best to make a note of them and then make a special effort to learn them.

■ One way of remembering the spelling of words that tend to trip you up is to group them together. This can help draw your attention to their similarities, or in some cases to their differences. Here are some examples:

suspend   suspense   suspension

press   repress   repression   impress   impression   suppress   suppression

compete   competitive   competition.

Activity

To round off this part of the unit, look at the words below and see if you are certain about their meaning and spelling. Use your dictionary to check you have the right meaning and test yourself on the spelling of each.

faction	recriminations	tribulations
inflexion	collaboration	refraction
fractious	corroboration	crenellations
crucial	remuneration	munitions
retribution	rendition	rehabilitation

Is it ie or ei?

If you ask anyone about spelling rules, they are more likely than not to say 'I before e, except after c', but this is only half the rule and if you only know the first half, it isn't very useful. The complete rule is:

I before e except after c

but only in words that rhyme with see.

For this rule to apply there must be a long **e** sound in a word.

If you say the following words aloud, you can hear the **e** sound, so the rule applies and it is **i** before **e**.

priest	achieve	besiege	shriek	grief	niece

In the next box it's **e** before **i** as **ei** follows **c**. If you read the words aloud you will be able to hear a long **e** sound in each.

conceive	receive	deceive	ceiling	perceive

Activity

In the words below the pattern is **ei**. This **ei** doesn't follow **c**, but there is no **e** sound in each word. What are the underlined sounds that you can hear in each word? Make a note of these.

1 w<u>ei</u>ght	2 th<u>ei</u>r	3 h<u>ei</u>ght
4 sl<u>ei</u>gh	5 h<u>ei</u>r	6 l<u>ei</u>sure
7 n<u>ei</u>ghbour	8 <u>ei</u>ght	9 h<u>ei</u>fer

You probably heard a long **a** sound like the **a** at the beginning of **apron** in: (1), (4), (7), (8). For words with an **ei** pattern *(unless* they are appearing after **c**) the most common sound for them to make is a long **a** sound (**apron**). In (2) and (5) you would hear the word **air**. In (3) you would hear a long **i** sound as at the beginning of **ice**. In (6) and (9) there is a short **e** sound as **e** makes at the beginning of **elephant**.

Review

Now check that you have met your targets for this unit. See if you can:

- Note down ways of spelling a hissing sound.

- What advice would you give someone about **tion** and **sion**?

- Try writing down the **ie/ei** rule.

You may not need to check up on yourself, but if you feel happier doing so go back through the unit and ensure that your responses to this review are correct.

STUDY WORDS

Targets

This unit will help you to:

→ recognise the importance of spelling in subjects other than English;

→ recognise where difficult spellings may occur in subjects;

→ identify particular spelling patterns that you need to work on;

→ develop ways of learning the spelling of complicated technical words.

In this unit you will be thinking about spelling technical words. By technical words we mean those words that are specific to a subject. For example, if you are studying a science, you will probably be presented with a large number of difficult technical words. We are going to look at those subjects where you might need special help with spelling. You will probably wish to work only through the activities connected to your own subject areas, but you may find it useful to look at the suggestions we make in each section. You may need to use your dictionary to check the meanings of some words we have given you in this unit.

Activity

Before you go further, think about the spelling of technical words within the subjects you are studying. Read through any essays or assignments you have written, and use the box below to list any technical words that you find difficult to spell.

(continued overleaf)

> If you cannot find words to list or cannot spot the difficulties, you may like to look at the examples below. Ring the parts of these words that you feel could cause you problems:
>
> | | | | |
> |---|---|---|---|
> | geography | history | biology | physics |
> | calcareous | Risorgimento | stimuli | pivot |
> | subterranean | utilitarianism | cytoplasm | aneroid |

Here are some reasons why technical words are likely to be difficult. Review your work on the activity above and place a tick next to those that seem to apply to you.

☐ Technical words are not in everyday use so we don't see them frequently enough to pick up the spelling easily.

☐ Technical words are sometimes long and complicated.

☐ Technical words are often taken from other languages.

☐ Sometimes letters within a technical word may make an unexpected sound.

☐ Technical words often have irregular patterns for plurals, etc.

Ways of tackling technical terms

If technical terms seem daunting, consider the following points:

■ You won't have to learn all the technical words for your subject at once. Work on a few at a time. You can use strategies to help yourself, for example breaking long words into smaller parts.

■ As you will probably have to adopt a slower reading style when studying, you can begin to look at new technical words more closely, building up a picture of each word.

■ If you make a point of copying down the word correctly each time, it will draw your attention to the spelling pattern.

Chemistry

Chemistry and biology probably involve the longest technical words, but long words might not always cause you difficulties. Many of these words will have been built up by adding on prefixes and endings, so you can learn them by taking the words apart. Take, for example:

chlorofluorocarbon.

You can easily get lost in this mammoth eighteen-letter word, but you can split it into smaller parts:

chloro fluoro carbon.

Each part is still a word in its own right but you can make each part even smaller:

ch loro flu oro car bon.

Activity

Look at these words and use the box below to suggest ways of splitting them:

phenolphthalein   sesquicarbonate   chromatography

polymerisation   efflorescence   monosaccharides

You will have decided to split the words in ways that you found most helpful. We would divide them as follows: phenolph–thalein; ses–qui–carbon–ate; chroma–tography; poly–meri–sation; ef–flor–escence; mono–sac–char–ides.

You may also have noticed that by splitting up words in this way you can cope more easily with difficult letter combinations, for example, the **cc** in **monosaccharides**.

Activity

Now underline the letter or letter combinations in the words below which might be problematic for you.

distillation   hydrolysis   malleable   covalent

catalyst   chloride   aluminium   ammonium

Our students would probably underline these letters: disti**ll**ation; hydrol**y**sis; mall**e**able; coval**e**nt; catal**y**st; **c**hloride; alum**iniu**m; a**mm**onium. If you underlined the same letters, you could deal with them by:

■ splitting the word between the double letters – distil–lation   am–monium (Unit 2 gives you more help with this);

■ remembering that **y** can have several sounds – hydrol**y**sis and catal**y**st;

■ using a memory aid, for example, saying 'two **y**s in **hydrolysis**' as you write the word or focus on the **y**s when you learn the word;

■ remembering the silent **h** in **chloride** by saying the word with a **ch** sound at the beginning or learning the word as part of a family – chloride, chlorate, chlorophyll, chlorine, etc.;

■ emphasising the **e** sound in **malleable** as you write the word each time;

■ trying a chant, for example, alu~min~i~um;

■ breaking the word up, for example, by looking for **mini** in alu**mini**um and remembering that there is a **u** on either side of it.

41

Biology

Many of the technical words in biology have come from Latin. Since they tend to be long and complicated, taking them apart may help you to spell them. You may also find it helpful to learn words in their word families:

trachea   **trache**oles   **trache**id

loco**cytes**   lympho**cytes**   thrombo**cytes**   erythro**cytes**   phago**cytes**.

Activity

Using your dictionary and biology textbooks, find word families which start with these letters.

epi	chi	meta

You may also find that when studying biology you need to think carefully about plural patterns, for example:

stimul**us** = singular   stimul**i** = plural.

Activity

Check the plurals of the following words in your dictionary. Then note them down in the right hand column.

singular	plural
fungus	
larva	
antenna	
trachea	
nucleus	
bacillus	
bacterium	

Your dictionary will have shown you that to make the plural of **fungus**, **bacillus** and **nucleus**, you remove the **us** and add **i**; for **larva**, **antenna** and **trachea** you add an **e**; **bacterium** becomes **bacteria**. When you come across a technical word that has an unusual ending, try to make a note of that word and see whether it fits into any pattern.

Physics

In physics you may not be concerned with such long words as in chemistry and biology but remember short words can still be tricky, for example:

fulcrum   (you may be undecided: one **l** or two?)

piv**o**t   (you may need to emphasise the **o**).

Activity

Look at these words and put a ring round the tricky points:

aneroid	decibels	vacuum	freon
helium	rheostat	neutral	viscous

We have underlined the points that you may need to consider: an<u>e</u>roid, deci<u>be</u>ls, vac<u>uu</u>m, fr<u>e</u>on, h<u>e</u>lium, r<u>h</u>eostat, n<u>eu</u>tral, visc<u>ou</u>s. Train yourself to spot the difficult part and focus on this point every time you use the word.

Tricky endings

Students are sometimes uncertain about **or**, **er** and **ar** endings:

generator   molecular   transformer.

Does the ending of each word sound the same?

Activity

Check the endings of the following words.

conduct __ __	accumulat __ __	radiat __ __
convect __ __	condens __ __	transist __ __
insulat __ __	resist __ __	reflect __ __

You will have seen that all these words have an **or** ending. You may find it helpful to group together other technical words which share the same endings.

History

In this subject you will have to make sure that you learn the correct spelling of the names of people, places, treaties, and battles, for example:

Chamberlain   Disraeli

Battle of Worcester   Culloden.

Foreign names and words may need special care:

Metternich   Weimar Republic   Lebensraum.

You may find that saying the word as it is spelt helps you with missing parts, silent letters or unexpected sounds. You may also find it helpful to keep a list of the names of people and places that are connected with the historical period you are studying. Sort out any that might be difficult to spell and find strategies for those words.

Activity

The following words are sometimes misspelt in history essays. Complete them by filling in the missing letters and then checking the words in your dictionary.

bourg _ _ _ sie	gove *rnme* nt	par *liam e* nt
perest _ _ _ ka	cont _ _ p _ _ _ r y	neg _ _ _ _ ti _ ns
camp _ _ _ n	man _ _ _ v _ e	mil _ t _ _ _ sm

Geography

Place names often cause spelling problems for geography students, for example:

Kirkcudbright   Gloucester   Leicester.

Activity

You may like to check that you can spell the names of:

the area surrounding the South Pole

the sea between Europe and Africa

the continent that includes New Zealand

the sea that lies between Central and South America

Check that you included a **c** in Anta**rc**tic; double **r** in Medite**rr**anean but one **r** and two **bs** in Ca**ribb**ean. Australasia can be split into Austral + asia.

The other words you may need to concentrate upon are those referring to physical features. Some will have such distinctive spellings that they may well be memorable:

oolitic   gneiss   mica-schist.

Others may give you more difficulties.

Activity

Look carefully at each word below. Then cover it up and see if you can write the word correctly. If you find you've made a mistake, ask yourself:

■   Is it important to know the correct spelling?

■   If so, could you learn it?

isthmus	glacial	tertiary	estuary
erosion	escarpment	sedimentary	moraine

Review

Now review whether this unit has helped you to think more carefully about the spelling of technical words.

■   Have you thought about ways that will help you to adopt a careful approach to the spelling of technical words?

■   Before passing work to your tutor or assessor, will you make a special spelling check of any technical words you have used?

■   Have you identified all the words in your subject that you should work on?

UNIT
10

REVIEWING PROGRESS

Targets

This unit will help you to:

→ review what you have achieved;

→ recall and use the various methods for learning spelling patterns;

→ think about where you go from here.

What have you achieved?

We hope you have enjoyed working through this material and that you've gained something from it. At the end of any course of study it's a good idea to take stock and to think about your achievements. We suggest you crystallise your thoughts by noting down what you feel you have gained. Set aside a good ten minutes for this, then compare notes with the comments below.

Here are some possibilities. You may have:

■ started to feel more positive about your spelling and better about writing;

■ identified the words you often make mistakes with and set about learning these;

■ become aware of the types of mistakes you make;

■ learnt new ways of memorising problem words;

■ developed a routine for learning new words;

■ gained more information about English spelling patterns.

Ways of remembering words

As you have worked through the units you have been offered advice about how to learn and remember certain spelling patterns. Although much of this advice has been specific to the type of word that you've been learning within the unit, some of it has been general advice about how you can improve your spelling.

Activity

Think about all the suggestions we have made. Then make a list in the box below of the points that you have found particularly helpful and will use in future with any problem words that you encounter.

We all need help learning certain words that we are confused by and we need to have a variety of strategies to call on. Often you need to put several of your strategies together to work on a particular word.

Activity

Now try out your strategies by working on the following words. We've selected words that people often have trouble spelling – particularly in exams.

yacht	fulfil	exhausted	accelerator
technology	conscious	itinerary	keenness
regrettable	resuscitation	recognition	integrity
pamphlet	responsibilities	critically	apparatus
vaccination	permanent	contemporary	velocity
pitifully	prominent	society	fluorescent
pronunciation	humorous	judicial	

We haven't given you any answers to this activity because the methods you choose will be the ones which are useful to you personally.

Where next?

Now that your spelling has improved, don't stop here. None of us is perfect at spelling; we all have our blind spots and occasional lapses. This spelling course is here for you to refer to when you need it. We also hope that it will have whetted your appetite and made you want to learn more about spelling. Below is a list of some more detailed books about spelling which may help you to follow up this interest.

Getting to Grips with Spelling, Catherine Hilton and Margaret Hyder, Letts Educational

A Guide to Better Spelling, A.M. Burt, Stanley Thornes

Learn to Spell, Walter D. Wright, James Nisbet

Spelling Matters, Bernard R. Sadler, Edward Arnold

Spelling it Out, Rhiannedd Pratley, BBC Books

Assignments in Punctuation and Spelling, Eric Williams, Edward Arnold

Good luck! We hope you will put your spelling to good use and enjoy writing more.

SPELLING

ASSIGNMENTS FOR TUTORIAL COMMENT

NATIONAL
EXTENSION
COLLEGE

Introduction

These assignments are intended for learners studying with an NEC tutor. Each of the assignments should be carried out at the point indicated. You should send an assignment to your tutor as soon as you have completed all its parts. Your tutor will mark your answers and give you personal help. He or she will also deal with any difficulties you meet, and help you to adapt the course to suit your own circumstances.

Treat each assignment as a further step to learning. Don't worry about making mistakes; the word 'error' originally meant 'wandering about looking for something'. It is through making errors that we learn things and find what it is that we are looking for. However, if you feel unsure of how to respond to a question, write to your tutor and ask for advice. While you are waiting for a reply, go on to the next Unit.

Bear in mind the contribution that your family and friends can make to your learning. Discuss ideas with them and if possible persuade them to read your assignments and comment on them before you send them to your tutor.

How to present your assignments

Please follow these instructions for all your assignments.

1   Leave a margin of one and a half inches (about 4cm) on the left side of the page and three inches (about 8cm) along the bottom. This space is for your tutor's comments.

2   If you are not typing your assignments, make sure that your handwriting is clear. Use pen not pencil.

3   Number each question clearly.

ASSIGNMENT A

Send this to your tutor when you have completed Unit 2

Part 1

Read this before you begin Unit 1

At the beginning of Unit 1 we ask you to make a note of words that you feel cause you problems or that you are uncertain about. When you have completed Units 1 and 2 we would like you to send an initial list to your tutor. Don't worry about whether you have spelt the words on your list correctly at this stage. Your tutor's aim will not be to mark your work but to advise you on ways of tackling problem areas.

Part 2

Read this before you begin Unit 2

Unit 2 looks at words with double letters that may cause you problems. On page 11 we ask you to list these. We would like you to send this initial list to your tutor when you have completed your work on Unit 2. You should accompany your list with a note of the ways you have identified of tackling these problem spellings. The list on page 11 'How to tackle double letters' should help you here, but you are welcome to mention other techniques if you find these helpful – either ones you have made up yourself or ideas taken from other sources.

Part 3

Read this when you have completed Unit 2 and the second part of this assignment.

When you send your tutor Parts 1 and 2 accompany these with a short note (100–200 words) introducing yourself to your tutor. You could say something about:

• your current studies or work

• why accurate spelling is important to you

• what you hope to gain from the course

• the dictionary you will be referring to as you work through this course

• any spelling difficulties you may have that you have not had the chance to raise in Parts 1 and 2.

ASSIGNMENT B

Send this assignment to your tutor when you have completed Unit 4

Part 1

Read this when you reach the end of Unit 3.

(a) Unit 3 suggests ways of dealing with words containing the letter Y. For the first part of this assignment we would like you to suggest the correct plural endings for the following words. Do this by:

• copying down the list below on a clean sheet of paper

• noting down next to each word its plural form.

We suggest that you do this without using a dictionary. This will enable your tutor to spot any errors and suggest ways of avoiding these in the future.

abbey	pony
estuary	quay
key	seminary
nanny	sherry
ploy	tray

(b) Unit 3 also discusses word endings. To put your learning into practice, add the ending shown in brackets to the following words. Note down both the original word and its revised form when you send your work to your tutor:

weary (some)	secretary (al)
convey (ing)	mercury (al)
deny (ed)	nasty (er)
drowsy (ness)	victory (ous)

Part 2

Complete this when you reach the end of Unit 4.

Unit 4 asks you to consider which word beginnings are a possible cause of problems for you. For this part of Assignment B we would like you to do two things:

(a) Send a note to your tutor of any word beginnings that you find confusing. If there are none, fine! But don't be reluctant to raise any queries with your tutor.

(b) Now see if you can suggest which letter – or letters – is missing in each of the following words. As before, list the completed words for your tutor to check – without consulting your dictionary:

d–cide	d–ssolve
d–duct	d–vorce
d–mote	—mediate
d–pict	—prove
d–ffuse	—famous
d–ploma	—finite

Don't forget to send all parts of your assignment to your tutor as soon as you have completed this final part.

ASSIGNMENT C

Send this assignment to your tutor when you have completed Unit 6.

(a) Units 5 and 6 deal with silent letters. For this assignment we would first like you to send your tutor a note of:

• any silent letters that you feel are continuing to concern you

• other examples where a silent 'e' is difficult to remember

• any queries you have over the use of silent letters in words

• the ways you have identified of tackling the spellings of words in which some
    letters are silent.

(b) This is also the point in the course where you may find it useful to take stock of your progress so far. We would like you to write a short letter to your tutor, reviewing your progress You should include something on:

• what you feel you have gained from the course so far

• any general points about spelling that you are continuing to find difficult.

Aim to write up to two sides of A4 (the size of this page).

ASSIGNMENT D

Send this assignment to your tutor when you have completed Unit 8.

Part 1

Complete this when you reach the end of Unit 7.

(a) Unit 7 looks at words containing **ph**. Make a note of at least five of these words that you need to use in your own work or study and which in the past you have been uncertain about. Add a note of how you intend to memorise these.

(b) Unit 7 also considers the use of **que** and **ch** for the 'k' sound in words. Without referring to the unit, can you recall – and note down:

   • which ending is pronounced in this way only when it occurs at the end of
      words?

   • which ending is pronounced in this way only when it occurs in the middle or
      at the beginning of words?

Part 2

Read this before you begin Unit 8

(a) The activity on page 36 asks you to decide whether a selection of words requires the combination **ci** or **ti** to make the 'shun' sound. When you carry out this activity, make your notes on a single side of A4 paper and retain this for sending on to your tutor with your responses to (b) and (c) below.

Tackle (b) and (c) below when you reach the end of Unit 8

(b) Now decide which combination, **xi**, **si, ti** or **ci** is needed to complete the following words. (Write out your list for your tutor to check.)

controver_al   obno_ous

deli_ous   quo_ent

impar_al   vi_ous

(c) Finally, we would like you to send to your tutor a brief summary in your own words of the rule that explains when to use **ie** and when to use **ei** in words.

Don't forget to send both parts of this assignment to your tutor now that you have completed Part 2.

ASSIGNMENT E

Send this to your tutor when you have completed Unit 10

Part 1

Complete this when you reach the end of Unit 9

Unit 9 looks at the vocabulary of specific subjects. Think about the writing you carry out as part of your work or studies. Do you need to use any specialist or technical words? Are there any words connected with your work or studies that regularly cause you difficulty? We would like you to note down for your tutor:

• up to ten such words

• how you plan to tackle the spelling of these words

• any queries you have about the use of specialist words.

Part 2

Complete this when you reach the end of Unit 10.

For the second part of your final assignment we would like you to return to the list of problem words that you compiled at the start of the course. Do they still present difficulties for you? Prepare a table summarising your progress. You could use the following headings:

Word   Can now spell   Uncertain – needs more practice

Add to this list any other words that you have felt unsure of while working through this course.

Finally, write a letter (up to 200 words) to your tutor reviewing the course. You should include something on:

• what you feel you have gained from it

• any further work you feel is still needed on your spelling

• what further studies or work you now plan to go on to.

Don't forget to send both parts of this assignment to your tutor now that you have completed Part 2.

Index